DATE DUE		12-12
DEC 3 0 2012			

The Urbana Free Library

To renew: call 217-367-4057
or go to "urbanafreelibrary.org"
and select "Renew/Request Items"

Rocks

ANN O. SQUIRE

Children's Press®
An Imprint of Scholastic Inc.
New York Toronto London Auckland Sydney
Mexico City New Delhi Hong Kong
Danbury, Connecticut

Content Consultant
Vicki Harder
Associate Professor
Department of Natural Sciences
Western New Mexico University
Silver City, New Mexico

Library of Congress Cataloging-in-Publication Data

Squire, Ann.
  Rocks/by Ann O. Squire.
     p. cm.—(A true book)
  Includes bibliographical references and index.
  ISBN 978-0-531-26145-3 (lib. bdg.) — ISBN 978-0-531-26253-5 (pbk.)
1. Mineralogy—Juvenile literature. I. Title.
  QE365.2.S66 2013
  552—dc23   2012003190

All rights reserved. Published in 2013 by Children's Press, an imprint of Scholastic Inc.
Printed in China 62
SCHOLASTIC, CHILDREN'S PRESS, A TRUE BOOK™, and associated logos are trademarks and/or registered trademarks of Scholastic Inc.
1 2 3 4 5 6 7 8 9 10 R 22 21 20 19 18 17 16 15 14 13

Front cover: A hiker in Lower Antelope Canyon, Arizona

Back cover: Mt. Rushmore, South Dakota

Find the Truth!

Everything you are about to read is true *except* for one of the sentences on this page.

Which one is **TRUE**?

T or F It is so hot deep inside the earth that some rocks melt.

T or F Most fossils are found in igneous rocks.

Find the answers in this book.

Contents

THE BIG TRUTH!

The Rocky Mountains

4 Rocks and People

Granite is one of the
most common rocks
on Earth.

Many of the world's tallest buildings are made partially of rock.

CHAPTER 1

Rocks Are Everywhere

Rocks come in all shapes and sizes. They can be huge, craggy boulders or tiny, smooth pebbles. Rocks were used to build New York City's Empire State Building. The grains of sand at the beach are made of rock. The roof of your house and the counters in your kitchen may be made of rock. The same is true for the sidewalks and roads in your town. In fact, Earth itself is a giant rock!

The Empire State Building stands 1,454 feet (443 meters) tall.

What Are Rocks?

Rocks are made up of minerals, which are substances that occur naturally in the ground. Combinations of minerals clump together to form rock. Different kinds of rocks have different characteristics. For example, we think of all rocks as being hard, but some are harder than others. Granite is a very hard rock, and limestone is much softer.

Softer rocks, such as marble, are often used to create statues and other artwork.

About 71 percent of Earth's crust is covered by oceans.

The earth's outer layer is called the crust.

Our Rocky Planet

Let's take a look at planet Earth, starting from the outside and working our way to the center. The earth's outer skin, the part we live on, is called the crust. It is made of **continental** and **oceanic** rock. The crust is about 45 miles (72 kilometers) thick underneath the continents. It is thinnest beneath the ocean floor, where the crust may be only about 3 to 5 miles (5 to 8 km) thick.

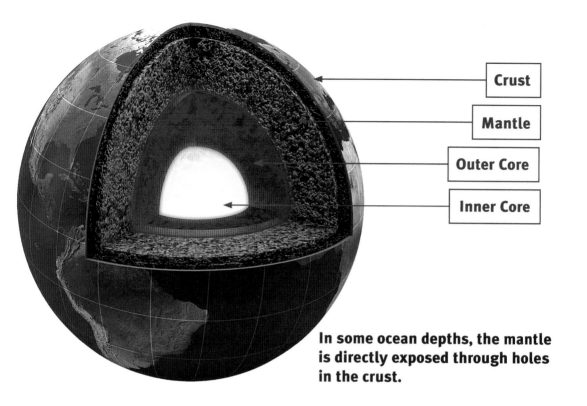

| Crust |

| Mantle |

| Outer Core |

| Inner Core |

In some ocean depths, the mantle is directly exposed through holes in the crust.

Beneath the Crust

Underneath the earth's crust is the mantle. This rocky layer is much thicker than the crust. It is up to 1,800 miles (2,897 km) thick. The temperature in the mantle is very hot. In some areas of the mantle, it is so hot that the rocks actually melt. The melted rocks form a molten material called **magma**. All of the world's rocks start out as magma.

A Broken Crust

Earth's crust is made up of pieces called tectonic plates that fit together like a puzzle. The plates are always moving, bumping, sliding past, or moving underneath each other. The area where two plates meet is called a plate boundary. This is usually marked by a fault line. The crust is weakest at this point. When plates move, an earthquake often occurs around the area of the plate boundary.

Earthquakes can cause incredible amounts of damage.

Journey to the Center of the Earth

Earth's core is divided into the outer and inner cores. The outer core consists of very dense, hot liquid rock. It is about 1,429 miles (2,300 km) thick and is thought to be around 7,950 degrees Fahrenheit (4,400 degrees Celsius). Scientists believe that the inner core is a solid ball of the metal iron and other elements. The ball is kept solid by an enormous amount of pressure. Temperatures are hottest here—up to 12,600°F (6,982°C).

Inner Core

Earth's inner core is about one-third the size of the moon.

Scientists use advanced technology to study the effects of earthquakes.

How Do We Know?

Since the 1960s, scientists have tried to drill through the earth's crust to take samples of the rock in the mantle. So far, they have not succeeded. If we cannot see the layers below the crust, how do we know about them? Scientists study the **seismic** waves created by earthquakes. Researchers can tell that the mantle is soft and jellylike compared to the rigid crust. Waves reflected from the earth's inner core tell us that the core is more solid.

Rocks change slowly over time.

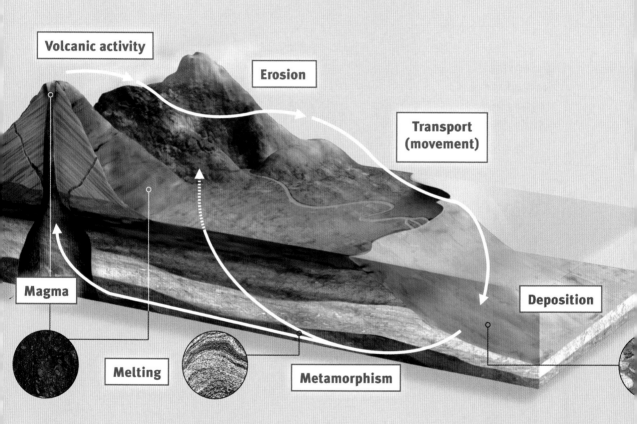

Volcanic activity

Erosion

Transport (movement)

Magma

Deposition

Melting

Metamorphism

The Rock Cycle

CHAPTER 2

Making Rocks

Rocks are always changing. Wind, weather, heat, and pressure constantly create and re-create different types of rocks. There are three main types of rocks. **Igneous** rocks get their start as magma. **Sedimentary** rocks begin as sediment, or tiny pieces of other rocks. Either of these types of rocks can be changed by intense heat and pressure into **metamorphic** rock. Metamorphic rocks can even be metamorphosed, or changed, into another type of metamorphic rock. This process of change is called the **rock cycle**.

Magma to Rock

Deep below the earth's surface, magma is constantly pushing upward against the crust. If there is a crack in the crust, the magma flows into it. The magma begins to cool and harden into rock. This happens because the temperature in the crust is lower than it is in the mantle.

Rocks that are formed in this way are called igneous rocks. The word *igneous* comes from the Latin word *ignis*, which means "fire."

The word "volcano" comes from Vulcan, the ancient Roman god of fire.

Sometimes magma reaches all the way to the surface.

Granite's crystals form slowly. They grow large as a result.

As magma cools, the minerals in it begin to **crystallize**. When magma cools very slowly in the earth's crust, large crystals form. Granite is a common igneous rock made from slowly cooling magma. Look at a chunk of rough granite or a slab of polished granite. It is very easy to identify the individual mineral crystals contained within.

Pumice is extremely light compared to most other rocks.

Volcanic Rocks

In some places, cracks in the crust are especially large. Magma works its way to the surface, creating a volcano. Magma that reaches the earth's surface in this way is called lava. Lava cools much more quickly than magma that is trapped underground, and it forms different kinds of igneous rocks. The crystals of these surface rocks are much smaller than those of the ones formed underground. Pumice and obsidian are two types of rock created by quickly cooling lava.

Pumice vs. Obsidian

Both pumice and obsidian cool so quickly that crystals do not have a chance to grow. Pumice is formed from frothy, bubble-filled lava. It is filled with holes and looks almost like a sponge. It is also very lightweight and floats on water. Obsidian is a shiny black glass. It forms from thick, pasty lava that contains very little water.

Extremely sharp surgical blades can be made from obsidian.

Sedimentary Rocks

Some cliffs and hillsides look as though they were made of hundreds of layers stacked on top of one another. That is what sedimentary rock looks like. This type of rock forms from tiny pieces of preexisting rock. The pieces can come from igneous, metamorphic, or even other sedimentary rocks.

Sedimentary layers can result in interesting striped patterns.

Sedimentary rock is the least common of the three rock types.

20

As water flows downward, it helps shape the rock formations that cover the earth's surface.

Turning to Stone

Sedimentary rock formation starts with natural forces such as wind, weather, and the movement of glaciers. Over time, these forces wear down rocks and mountains, grinding them up into tiny pieces called sediment. The sediment is carried away by wind, water, or ice. It settles in all sorts of environments. As layers of sediment build up, pressure from the top layers squeezes the deeper layers until those deeper layers turn to stone.

Each layer of sedimentary rock contains important information that scientists can use to learn about the earth's past.

Looking at the Past

Many sedimentary rocks have bands in a variety of colors. These bands can tell scientists about the environment in which the sediment was originally deposited. For example, red bands of rock contain iron that rusted. Rusting requires oxygen, which means the rock formed on land. Black rocks contain a lot of organic material left by plants and animals. This indicates the rock probably formed deep underwater.

Finding Fossils

Limestone and shale are common types of sedimentary rock. It is in these rocks that scientists often find fossils of animals and plants that lived in prehistoric times. Fossils are rarely found in igneous rock. They are never found in metamorphic rock. Fossils would have been destroyed by the high heat and intense pressure that had changed sedimentary rock into metamorphic rock.

Scientists work carefully so they don't damage fossils as they remove them from rock layers.

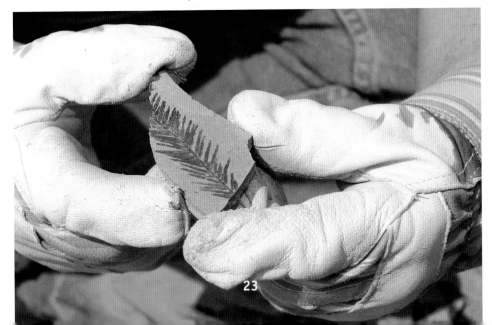

Metamorphic Rock

Any rock can be changed by heat and pressure into the third type of rock: metamorphic rock. When magma intrudes, or flows into, cracks in the earth's crust, it heats all the rocks nearby. If the area becomes hot enough, the surrounding rock can actually change. Limestone is a soft, sedimentary rock that turns into marble when the surrounding temperature is very high. In the same way, sandstone rich in quartz turns into a harder rock called quartzite.

Quartzite is often used to make roofing and flooring.

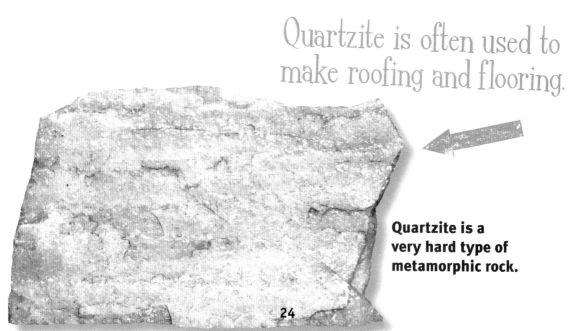

Quartzite is a very hard type of metamorphic rock.

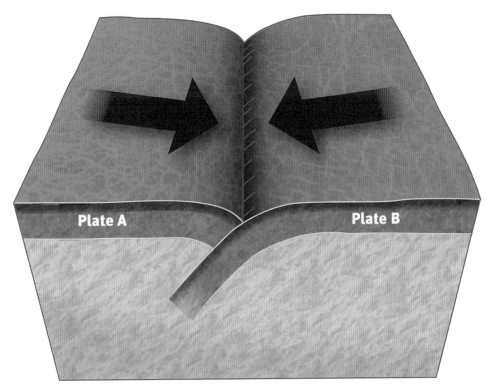

Plate A

Plate B

Rocks can be changed when plates push against each other.

Under Pressure

Rocks can also be changed by pressure. The plates that make up Earth's crust are constantly moving, bending, folding, and pushing against the plates nearby. When this happens, it puts great pressure on the rocks that make up the plates. This extreme pressure can change the rocks into metamorphic rock.

Gneiss is often used to create gravestones.

Granite (left) looks different from gneiss (right).

It is through intense pressure that granite, an igneous rock, turns into a metamorphic rock called gneiss. Pressure is also responsible for turning the sedimentary rock shale into slate, a metamorphic rock. When rocks are changed by heat and pressure, their appearance and internal crystal structure can change. The new rock may be made of the same materials as the original, but the density, smoothness, and other aspects of the rock have dramatically changed.

The Cycle Continues

Metamorphic, sedimentary, and igneous rocks can become buried deep beneath the earth's surface. The deeper they go, the more heat and pressure the rocks experience. Under the right conditions, the rocks melt into magma. The magma can then move back up toward the surface to cool and form igneous rock. This starts the rock cycle over again.

Magma, seen here in the form of lava, cools quickly after reaching the earth's surface.

The Grand Canyon is one of the most famous landmarks in the United States.

CHAPTER 3

Reshaping Rocks

The surface of the earth is rough and uneven. Mountains tower high above low valleys and deep oceans. Canyons cut through a landscape that is filled with strange, rocky shapes. How does this happen? The same forces that change one type of rock into another also help shape the surface of our planet.

 Some parts of the Grand Canyon are more than a mile deep.

Making Mountains

As the plates that make up earth's crust move and shift, they create heat and pressure. This can turn igneous and sedimentary rock into metamorphic rock. The movement can also create mountains. When two plates push against each other hard enough, the rocks fold and are forced upward to form mountain ranges. Valleys are created as water carries away the more easily **eroded** materials, leaving low areas between mountains.

The Great Rift Valley in East Africa was formed by the combined forces of plate movement and erosion.

Erosion and weathering can help create breathtaking rock formations.

Wind and Weather

Even as mountains form, they begin to break down.
Pounded by rain and wind, the rocks are worn away.
They turn into tiny pieces of sediment that will be
the building blocks of new sedimentary rock. When
small pieces of sediment are carried away by wind
or water, the process is called erosion.

Mammoth Cave is filled with fascinating rock shapes.

Weathering and erosion have created some amazing sights. The deep gorges and steep cliffs of the Grand Canyon were a result of the Colorado River cutting through sedimentary rock. Spectacular natural arches in Utah are the result of wind, rain, freezing, and thawing. Underground cavities such as Kentucky's Mammoth Cave were formed as water dissolved soft limestone.

Air Pollution and Acid Rain

Human activities can affect the condition of rocks. In places where there are many cars and factories, air pollution can occur. Air pollution is harmful to living things, and it can also harm stone buildings. India's Taj Mahal is made of white marble. Pollution from factories and traffic is leaving dirty stains on the building and cracks in its walls. Pollution also increases the amount of acid in rainwater, which can damage buildings made of soft stone.

The outside of the Taj Mahal is being worn away slowly by the effects of pollution.

33

Rocks From Outer Space

Not all rocks were made on Earth. Space is full of rocky asteroids and meteoroids. Scientists believe that asteroids, the biggest of these rocks, are left over from the formation of the solar system. Most asteroids are found between the orbits of Jupiter and Mars.

Meteoroids are much smaller than asteroids, but most were created the same way. Others broke off of the moon or other planets. Shooting stars are meteoroids that enter Earth's atmosphere. They burn up as they pass through the atmosphere, leaving a fiery trail. Sometimes, a meteoroid survives its trip and lands on Earth. These rocks from space are then called meteorites.

Meteorites can tell us a lot about distant planets. In 1984, scientists found a meteorite that they believe came from Mars. While studying it, they discovered clues that there might once have been life on that planet. They also found markings that might be tiny, fossilized organisms.

Many cosmetics are made from rocks.

CHAPTER 4

Rocks and People

People have depended on rocks for thousands of years. Stones are used to make buildings, roads, and sculptures. Rocks have been turned into tools for activities such as hunting, spinning yarn, and grinding grain. They have even been used as ingredients for dyes and makeup. It is hard to think of an area of human life that doesn't involve rocks!

When ground into very fine powders, many rocks can provide coloring in cosmetics.

Tools From Stone

Early humans made the first stone tools more than 3.2 million years ago. Spear points, axes, and early knives are some of the tools that have been found. A stone weight on the end of a pointed stick made a good tool for digging. Two stones could be rubbed against each other to grind corn and other grains. A flat rock on a pointed stick made a spindle that could be used to spin yarn.

A Rocky Timeline

4.6 billion years ago
Earth forms as a solid planet.

70 million to 40 million years ago
The Rocky Mountains begin to form.

6 million to 5 million years ago
The Colorado River begins to create the Grand Canyon.

Building Blocks

Throughout history, some of the most famous buildings in the world have been made of stone. The pyramids of Egypt are built of limestone, and so is Notre Dame Cathedral in Paris, France. Limestone and marble were used to construct the Parthenon in Greece. Granite and other rocks make up the 5,500-mile-long (8,850 km) Great Wall of China. If you look around your town or city, you're sure to find many buildings made of stone.

3.2 million years ago
Early humans make the first stone tools.

2011 CE
Newly created igneous rocks float in the ocean following the eruption of an underwater volcano in the Canary Islands.

Man-made Stone

Concrete and brick are two of the most popular building materials today. Both of them come from stone. Concrete is made of ground limestone mixed with sand, gravel, cement, and water. When it sets, it forms a very strong building stone. Sidewalks are made of concrete. Bricks are made of clay, a material that contains small pieces of weathered rock. Clay is soft when mixed with water. But after baking it at a high heat, it forms a hard, strong brick.

Some people continue to make handmade bricks from clay or mud.

40

Azurite (blue minerals above) and malachite (green minerals above) were once important ingredients in paints and dyes.

Creating Color

Before paint was available, people made colored powders out of crushed or ground rocks and minerals. Azurite could be ground to a rich, blue powder, and malachite created a bright green. When mixed with liquid, these powders could be used as paint. Powdered malachite was also used in ancient Egypt as eye makeup. Red ochre, a type of clay, was ground and used on the face and lips.

You can find rocks almost everywhere you look.

Important Stones

Rocks are an important part of everyday life. Rocks provide us the tools as well as the materials to build. They give us sturdy shelters, sidewalks, and roads. They even provide color to our world. Rocks make up the very planet we live on. Next time you walk down the street, see if you can spot all the rocks around you. You are surrounded! ★

Understanding Geodes

A geode is an amazing rock. On the outside, it looks like a dull, round rock. But inside, there may be sparkling crystals. Geodes are thought to start out as a bubble in volcanic rock or a hollow area in sedimentary rock. Water and dissolved minerals seep in and harden into an outer shell. The minerals continue to crystallize on the inner walls of the shell. Geodes may contain quartz, amethyst, and other minerals.

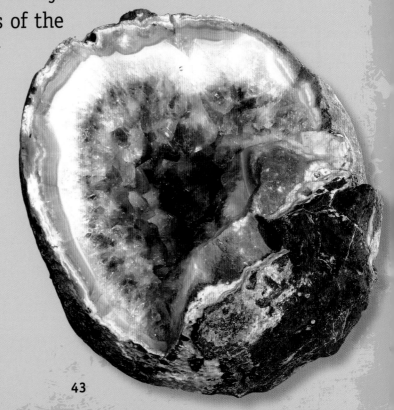

True Statistics

Age of the world's oldest sedimentary rocks: 3.9 billion years old

Time it takes for igneous rock to form: As little as a few seconds

Deepest hole ever drilled into the earth: 7.6 mi. (12.2 km)

Height of Mauna Loa, the largest volcano on Earth: 13,677 ft. (4,168.7 m) above sea level

Weight of the largest meteorite ever found on Earth: 60 tons (54 metric tons)

Age of the Acasta gneiss in Canada, the world's oldest metamorphic rock: More than 4 billion years old

Did you find the truth?

T It is so hot deep inside the earth that some rocks melt.

F Most fossils are found in igneous rocks.

Resources

Books

Ganeri, Anita. *Eruption! The Story of Volcanoes*. New York: DK Publishing, 2010.

Gray, Susan H. *Geology: The Study of Rocks*. New York: Children's Press, 2012.

Morgan, Sally. *Rocks*. Mankato, MN: Smart Apple Media, 2012.

Tomecek, Steve. *Everything Rocks and Minerals*. Washington, DC: National Geographic, 2010.

Visit this Scholastic Web site for more information on rocks:
★ www.factsfornow.scholastic.com
Enter the keyword **Rocks**

Important Words

continental (kahn-tuh-NEN-tuhl) — having to do with one of the seven large landmasses of the earth

crystallize (KRIS-tuh-lize) — to form crystals

eroded (ir-RODE-id) — worn away by water, wind, or glacial ice

igneous (IG-nee-uhs) — produced by great heat or by a volcano

magma (MAG-muh) — melted rock found beneath the earth's surface

metamorphic (met-uh-MOR-fik) — of or having to do with rock that is formed by pressure and heat

oceanic (oh-shee-AN-ik) — of or having to do with the mass of saltwater that covers about 71 percent of the earth's surface

rock cycle (ROK SYE-kuhl) — process in which rocks are made, broken down, and re-formed into new rocks

sedimentary (sed-uh-MEN-tur-ee) — of or having to do with rock that is formed by layers of sediment that have been pressed together

seismic (SIZE-mik) — of or having to do with waves of movements beneath the earth's surface

Index

Page numbers in **bold** indicate illustrations

About the Author

Ann O. Squire is a psychologist and an animal behaviorist. Before becoming a writer, she studied the behavior of rats, tropical fish in the Caribbean, and electric fish from Central Africa. Her favorite part of being a writer is the chance to learn as much as she can about all sorts of topics. In addition to *Gemstones*, *Fossils*, *Rocks*, and *Minerals*, Dr. Squire has written about many different animals, from lemmings to leopards and cicadas to cheetahs. She lives in Katonah, New York.